BUDDHA'S LITTLE
INSTRUCTION BOOK

BUDDHA'S LITTLE

Bantam Books *New York • Toronto • London • Sydney • Auckland*

INSTRUCTION BOOK

Jack Kornfield

BUDDHA'S LITTLE INSTRUCTION BOOK
A Bantam Book / June 1994
Designed and produced by David Bullen, with Michael Katz

LIBRARY OF CONGRESS CATALOGING-IN-PUBLICATION DATA
Kornfield, Jack, 1945–
    Buddha's little instruction book / Jack Kornfield.
        p.   cm.
    ISBN 0-553-37385-4
    1. Religious life—Buddhism.   I. Title
BQ5405.K67   1994
294.3´444—dc20   93-41545
                                                    CIP

Published simultaneously in the United States and Canada

Bantam Books are published by Bantam Books, a division of Bantam Doubleday Dell Publishing Group,
Inc. Its trademark, consisting of the words "Bantam Books" and the portrayal of a rooster, is Registered
in U.S. Patent and Trademark Office and in other countries. Marca Registrada. Bantam Books, 1540
Broadway, New York, New York, 10036.

PRINTED IN THE UNITED STATES OF AMERICA
0 9 8 7

The following words of wisdom come from the teachings of the Buddha and those meditation masters who have followed the Buddha's path of happiness. The simple verses in this book explore the themes of individual awareness and kindness, wise relationships, and the interconnection of all beings. At their heart they simply remind us that we too can live with the wakefulness and compassion of a Buddha.

In the back of the book is a section called "The Art of Meditation." It includes six meditations to quiet your mind and open your heart in the midst of everyday life.

May these words and practices bring you inspiration, wisdom, and delight.

Live every act fully, as if it were your last.

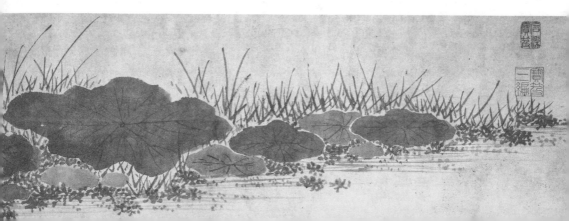

Love in the past is only a memory. Love in the future is a fantasy.
Only here and now can we truly love.

Most of the sorrows of the earth humans cause for themselves.

Even loss and betrayal can bring us awakening.

Words have the power to destroy or heal.

When words are both true and kind, they can change our world.

Every wakeful step, every mindful act is the direct path to awakening.
Wherever you go, there you are.

Our own worst enemy cannot harm us as much as our unwise *thoughts. No one can help us as much as our own compassionate thoughts.*

In one's family, respect and listening are the source of harmony.

To give your cow or sheep a large, spacious meadow is the best way to control him.

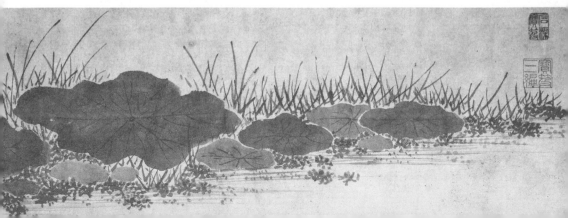

To open our own heart like a Buddha, we must embrace the ten thousand joys and the ten thousand sorrows.

The heart is like a garden. It can grow compassion or fear, resentment or love. What seeds will you plant there?

*True freedom comes when we follow our Buddha nature,
the natural goodness of our heart.*

Do not blindly believe what others say, even the Buddha. See for yourself what brings contentment, clarity, and peace. That is the path for you to follow.

Wherever you live is your temple if you treat it like one.

Though we often live unconsciously, "on automatic pilot," every one of us can learn to be awake. It just takes practice.

The mind contains all possibilities.

If you can't find the truth right where you are, where else do you think you will find it?

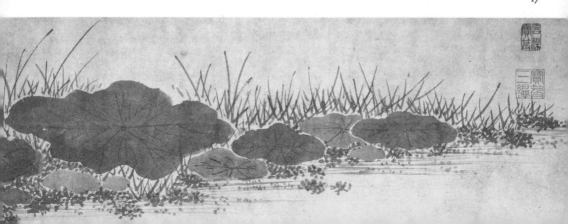

Life is as fleeting as a rainbow, a flash of lightning, a star at dawn.

Knowing this, how can you quarrel?

Hatred never ceases by hatred; by love alone is it healed.
This is the ancient and eternal law.

Victory creates hatred, defeat creates suffering. Those who are wise strive for neither victory nor defeat.

Let yourself be open and life will be easier. A spoon of salt in a glass of water makes the water undrinkable. A spoon of salt in a lake is almost unnoticed.

Weigh the true advantages of forgiveness and resentment to the heart. Then choose.

In the beginner's mind there are many possibilities, in the expert's mind there are few.

Happiness comes when your work and words are of benefit to yourself and others.

We are not independent but interdependent.

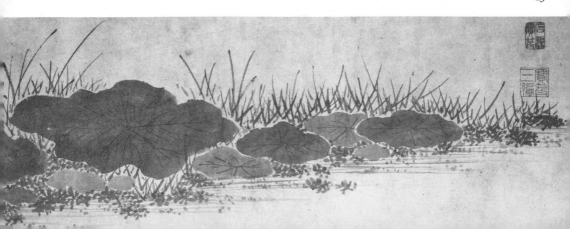

Spiritual life should include a great measure of common sense.

We can be spacious, yet full of loving kindness; full of compassion, yet serene. Live like the strings of a fine instrument—not too taut and not too loose.

If your compassion does not include yourself, it is incomplete.

Good-humored patience is necessary with mischievous children
and your own mind.

Life is so hard, how can we be anything but kind?

Our sorrows and wounds are healed only when we touch them with compassion.

Everything in moderation, including moderation.

There is only one time when it is essential to awaken.

That time is now.

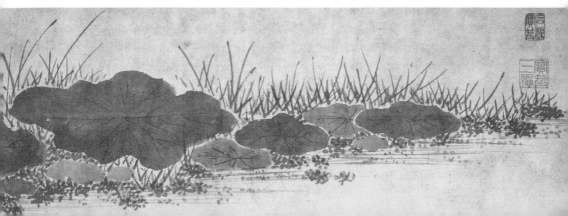

Through our senses the world appears. Through our reactions we create delusions. Without reactions the world becomes clear.

It is not our preferences that cause problems but our attachment to them.

Joy comes not through possession or ownership but through a wise
and loving heart.

The more fully we give our energy, the more it returns to us.

Health is the greatest gift, contentment the greatest wealth,
faithfulness the best relationship.

The trouble is that you think you have time.

Blessings come from care, troubles from carelessness.

If you do not care for each other, who will care for you?

Avoid the company of deluded people when you can.

When you cannot, keep your own counsel.

When leading, be generous with the community, honorable in action, sincere in your words. As for the rest, do not be concerned.

In business, reinvest a portion of all you make, keep a portion for your use, save a portion for those in need.

Whatever we cultivate in times of ease, we gather as strength for times of change.

Learn to respond, not react.

N*o matter how difficult the past, you can always begin again today.*

Our body is precious. It is our vehicle for awakening.

Treat it with care.

When you eat, eat slowly and listen to your body. Let your stomach tell you when to stop, not your eyes or your tongue.

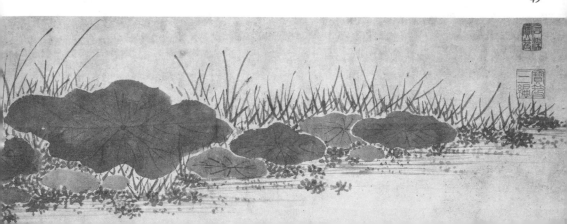

An upright posture and a few relaxed breaths can make a great difference.

We do not need more knowledge but more wisdom.
Wisdom comes from our own attention.

There are no holy places and no holy people, only holy moments,
only moments of wisdom.

When asked, *"Are you a god or a man?" the Buddha replied,*

"I am awake."

Whoever sees the truth sees the Buddha.

Desire blinds us, like the pickpocket who sees only the saint's pockets.

Not getting what you desire and getting what you desire can both be disappointing.

When wishes are few, the heart is happy. When desire ends,
there is peace.

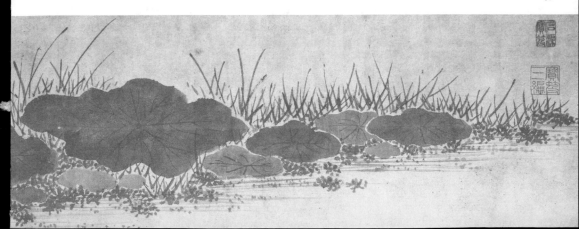

That which is timeless is found now.

As *you travel through life, offer good wishes to each being you meet.*

Just as driving on the right side of the road gives us the freedom to go anywhere, so accepting the natural law of constant change is our route to freedom.

Whatever path of action you find that brings good and happiness to all, follow this way like the moon in the path of the stars.

In wisdom be a lamp, a light unto yourself.

Karma can change life like the swish of a horse's tail.

Inner freedom is not guided by our efforts; it comes from seeing
what is true.

When you walk, just walk; when you eat, just eat.

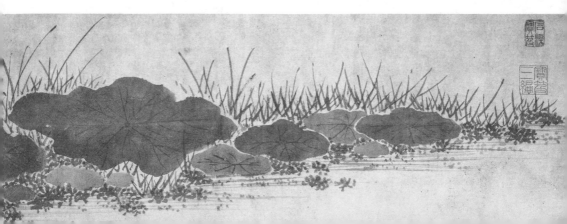

Don't keep searching for the truth, just let go of your opinions.

To meditate is to listen with a receptive heart.

Everything that has a beginning has an ending.
Make your peace with that and all will be well.

Stay centered, do not overstretch. Extend from your center, return to your center.

Take *time every day to sit quietly and listen.*

I*f you know about the power of a generous heart, you will not let a single meal pass without giving to others.*

Like the mother of the world, touch each being as your beloved child.

Harm no other beings. *They are just your brothers and sisters.*

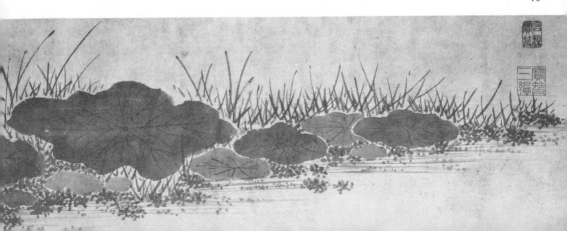

Learn to let go. That is the key to happiness.

*J*oy and openness come from our own contented heart.

To awaken, sit calmly, letting each breath clear your mind and
open your heart.

Just as a snake sheds its skin, we must shed our past over and over again.

n life we cannot avoid change, we cannot avoid loss. Freedom and happiness are found in the flexibility and ease with which we move through change.

Each morning we are born again.

What we do today is what matters most.

As you walk and eat and travel, be where you are.
Otherwise you will miss most of your life.

To know the way and not practice is to be a soup ladle in the pot
and not taste the flavor of the soup.

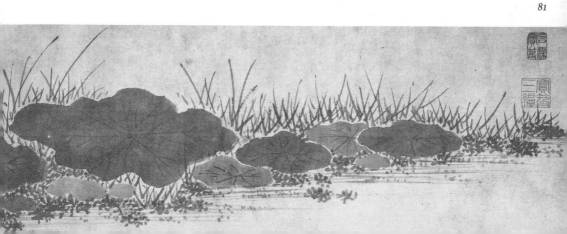

Treat others with justice and respect. In the long run, how you treat others will be how they treat you.

Imagine that every person in the world is enlightened but you.
They are all your teachers, each doing just the right things to help
you learn perfect patience, perfect wisdom, perfect compassion.

All *things are like a river. We never enter the same river twice.*

In the end these things matter most: How well did you love? How fully did you live? How deeply did you learn to let go?

raise and blame, gain and loss, pleasure and sorrow come and go like the wind. To be happy, rest like a great tree in the midst of them all.

The only way to bring peace to the earth is to learn to make our own life peaceful.

Even death is not to be feared by one who has lived wisely.

Neither fire nor wind, birth nor death can erase our good deeds.

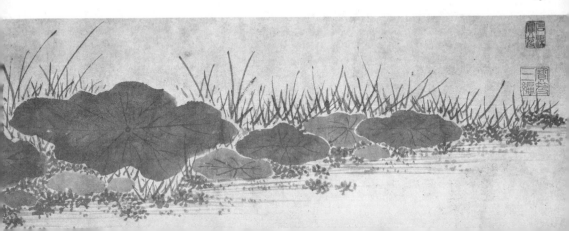

Ｎo one outside ourselves can rule us inwardly. When we know this,
we become free.

Fear is always an anticipation of what has not yet come. Our fear and separation are great, but the truth of our connection is greater still.

There is the path of fear and the path of love.

Which will we follow?

Every life has a measure of sorrow. Sometimes it is this that awakens us.

Strength and justice are the products of a steady heart.

Calm and compassion are so precious. Make sure not to lose them through intoxication.

Forgiveness is primarily for our own sake, so that we no longer carry the burden of resentment. But to forgive does not mean we will allow injustice again.

We inter-breathe with the rain forests, we drink from the oceans. They are part of our own body.

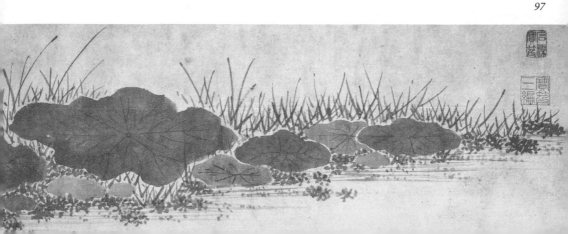

Roses become compost; compost feeds the garden for the growth of new roses.

We do not possess our home, our children, or even our own body.
They are only given to us for a short while to treat with care and
respect.

Even our anger can be held with a heart of kindness.

In conflict there is another way. Imagine that you were the Buddha; how would you solve it? (P.S. Who else could the Buddha be?)

What has been long neglected cannot be restored immediately. Fruit falls from the tree when it is ripe. The way cannot be forced.

Do not seek perfection in a changing world.

Instead, perfect your love.

Simplicity brings more happiness than complexity.

The greatest protection is a loving heart. Protecting yourself, you protect others. Protecting others, you protect yourself.

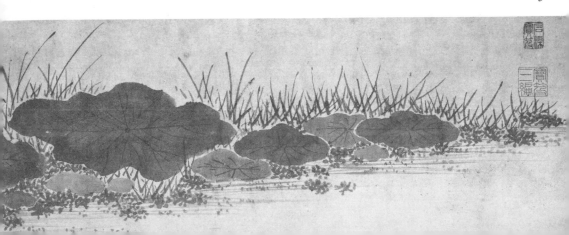

Generosity brings joy; honesty brings peace.

$\mathbf{D}$o not judge yourself harshly. Without mercy for ourselves we cannot love the world.

A *day spent judging another is a painful day. A day spent judging yourself is a painful day. You don't have to believe your judgments; they're simply an old habit.*

In times of difficulty take refuge in compassion and truth.

As rain falls on the just and the unjust alike, let your heart be untroubled by judgments and let your kindness rain on all.

At the bottom of things, most people want to be understood
and appreciated.

If we could see the miracle of a single flower clearly, our whole life would change.

There is no fire greater than greed and hatred.

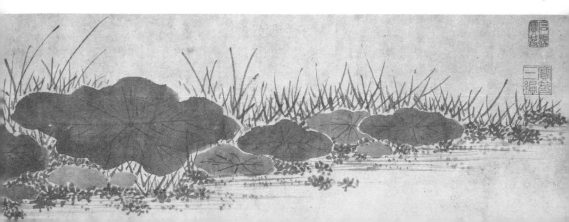

Life lives on life. We all eat and are eaten. When we forget this, we cry; when we remember this, we can nourish one another.

If you are poor, live wisely. If you have riches, live wisely. It is not your station in life but your heart that brings blessings.

Karma means you don't get away with anything.

When you meditate, sit with the dignity of a king or queen; when
you move through your day, remain centered in this dignity.

Let your mind become clear like a still forest pool.

If you let cloudy water settle, it will become clear. If you let your upset mind settle, your course will also become clear.

If you take care of each moment, you will take care of all time.

Some days we feel like strangers. When our heart opens, we will realize that we belong just here.

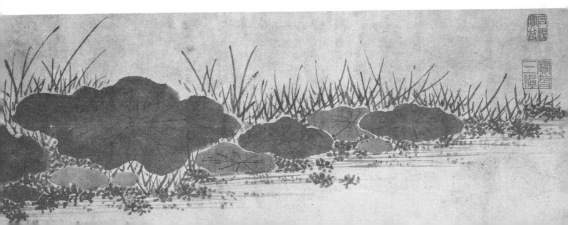

Things to do today: *Exhale, inhale, exhale. Ahhhh.*

If you wish to know the divine, feel the wind on your face and the warm sun on your hand.

Those who are awake live in a state of constant amazement.

THE ART OF MEDITATION

The following six meditations are traditional and simple practices for awakening a clear mind and a wise and open heart. The art of meditation teaches us to relax and remain alert in the midst of the problems and the joys of life. It allows us to rest in the moment with ease and respond to life with compassion.

A SITTING MEDITATION

Let Your Mind Settle Like a Clear Forest Pool

To begin meditation, select a quiet time and place. Be seated on a cushion or chair, taking an erect yet relaxed posture. Let yourself sit upright with the quiet dignity of a king or queen. Close your eyes gently and begin by bringing a full, present attention to whatever you feel within you and around you. Let your mind be spacious and your heart be kind and soft.

As you sit, feel the sensations of your body. Then notice what sounds and feelings, thoughts and expectations are present. Allow them all to come and go, to rise and fall like the waves of the ocean. Be aware of the waves and rest seated in the midst of them. Allow yourself to become more and more still.

In the center of all these waves, feel your breathing, your life-breath. Let your attention feel the in and out breathing wherever you notice it, as coolness or tingling in the nose or throat, as a rising and falling of your chest or abdomen. Relax and softly rest your attention on each breath, feeling the movement in a steady easy way. Let the breath breathe itself in any rhythm, long or short, soft or deep. As you feel each breath, concentrate and settle into its movement. Let all other sounds and sensations, thoughts and feelings continue to come and go like waves in the background.

After a few breaths, your attention may be carried away by one of the waves of thoughts or memories, by body sensations or sounds. Whenever you notice you have been carried away for a time, acknowledge the wave that has done so by softly giving it a name such as "planning," "remembering," "itching," "restless." Then let it pass and gently return to the breath. Some waves will take a long time to pass, others will be short. Certain thoughts or feelings will be painful, others will be pleasurable. Whatever they are, let them be.

At some sittings you will be able to return to your breath easily. At other times in your meditation you will mostly be aware of body sensations or of plans or thoughts. Either way is fine. No matter what you experience, be aware of it, let it come and go, and rest at ease in the midst of it all. After you have sat for twenty or thirty minutes in this way, open your eyes and look around you before you get up. Then as you move try to allow the same spirit of awareness to go with you into the activities of your day

The art of meditation is simple but not always easy. It thrives on practice and a kind and spacious heart. If you do this simple practice of sitting with awareness every day, you will gradually grow in centeredness and understanding.

A WALKING MEDITATION

When You Walk, Just Walk

The natural ease of walking can be used as a direct and simple way to bring centeredness and peace into our life. Walking becomes a meditation when we bring a careful and present attention to each step we take. Walking becomes a meditation when we feel ourselves fully here on the earth.

To learn walking meditation, select a place to walk back and forth at a leisurely rate, fifteen to thirty paces in length. Stand at the end of this "walking path." Feel your feet on the floor, on the earth. Sense the environment around you. Be aware of yourself and your surroundings until you feel quiet and composed. Then begin to walk. Focus your attention on your body, feeling each step as you lift your foot and place it back on the earth. As you sense each step, return your foot to the earth with care.

Walk upright in a relaxed and dignified fashion. When you get to the end of your path, pause briefly and then turn around. Stand and center yourself then and be aware of the first step as you begin again. You can walk at whatever speed keeps you most present.

Walk with careful attention to each step for fifteen or twenty minutes. Usually when we walk we are distracted by a hundred other things. As you walk in meditation, try to let the thoughts and images that arise remain in the background. Even so, you will regularly get carried away by thoughts. When this happens, simply stop walking and be aware of the thoughts. Then quietly re-center yourself and take the next step. Keep coming back to your footsteps in this simple way. At times you may wish to do a period of walking meditation alone. On other days you might walk for ten or fifteen minutes before beginning a sitting meditation.

After some practice you can learn to use walking meditation to calm and collect yourself, to become truly present in your body. You can extend this walking practice in informal ways, when you go shopping, when you walk down the street or to and from your car. You can learn to enjoy walking for its own sake instead of combining it with the usual planning and thinking. In this simple way you can move through life wakefully, with your whole body, heart, and mind together in harmony.

AN EATING MEDITATION

When You Eat, Just Eat

Eating meditation is a way to learn to eat with a respectful attention to your food and your body. It is easiest to begin in silence, although with practice you can learn to eat mindfully in any circumstance.

To start eating meditation, place your food in front of you and sit quietly. Reflect on the source of the food and recite any simple prayer of gratitude or blessing that comes naturally. Then be still for a few moments. Look carefully at the food. Be aware of your body and especially of your own feelings of hunger. Notice how you feel about putting this particular food into your body at this moment.

When you feel fully present and connected with yourself, begin to eat slowly. In a relaxed way be aware of each aspect of eating. Be aware of lifting the food to your mouth, of chewing, of tasting, of swallowing. Notice if you feel hurried. Take your time, taste each bite carefully. Be aware of the flavors, the textures, the feelings that arise with each mouthful. Pause for a moment before the next bite. Continue your meal with this same mindful attention to everything you eat, until you come to the end.

Notice when you start to feel full. Your stomach may tell you it is full first, even when your tongue or eyes want more. Your thoughts may tell you to finish everything on your plate, or that you are eating too much. If you can, don't follow these habits but listen to your whole body. Let yourself be guided by this attention. Practice this eating meditation when you can during the week. Even one meal eaten this way is a wonderful reminder of a mindful life.

LOVING KINDNESS MEDITATION

With a loving heart as the background, all that we attempt, all that we encounter will open and flow more easily. Loving kindness meditation uses phrases, images, and feelings to evoke a loving kindness and friendliness toward oneself and others. It is best to begin this practice by meditating for fifteen or twenty minutes daily in a quiet place.

Sit in a comfortable fashion. Let your body rest and be relaxed. Let your heart be soft, letting go of plans and preoccupations. Then begin to recite inwardly the following phrases directed to yourself. You begin with yourself because without loving yourself it is almost impossible to love others.

> *May I be filled with loving kindness.*
> *May I be well.*
> *May I be peaceful and at ease.*
> *May I be happy.*

As you repeat these phrases, you can picture yourself as a young and beloved child, or sense yourself as you are now, held in a heart of loving kindness. Adjust the words and images in any way you need to find the exact phrases that best open your heart of kindness. Repeat the phrases over and over again, letting the feelings permeate your body and mind. Practice this meditation for a number of weeks, until the sense of loving kindness for yourself grows.

Be aware that this meditation may at times feel mechanical or awkward or even bring up feelings contrary to loving kindness, feelings of irritation and anger. If this happens, it is especially important to be patient and kind toward yourself, allowing whatever arises to be received in a spirit of friendliness and kind affection.

When you feel you have established some sense of loving kindness, you can then expand your meditation to include others in the same meditation period. After focusing on yourself choose someone in your life who has truly cared for you. Picture this person and carefully recite the same phrases: *May he/may she be filled with loving kindness,* and so forth. When loving kindness for this person has developed, begin to include other people you love in the meditation, picturing each one and reciting the same phrases, evoking a sense of loving kindness for them.

After this you can include others: friends, community members, neighbors, people everywhere, animals, all beings, the whole earth. Then you can even include the difficult people in your life, wishing that they too be filled with loving kindness and peace. In the course of twenty minutes your meditation can open from yourself, to loved ones, to all beings everywhere.

Loving kindness can be practiced anywhere. You can use this meditation in traffic jams, in buses and airplanes. As you silently practice this meditation among people, you will immediately feel a wonderful connection with them—the power of loving kindness. It will calm your life and keep you connected to your heart.

FORGIVENESS MEDITATION

The act of forgiveness is one of the great gifts of spiritual life. It enables us and the world to be released from the sorrows of the past. Forgiveness is an act of the heart, a movement to let go of the resentment and outrage that we have carried for too long. It eases the burden of pain in our heart. To forgive does not mean we condone the misdeeds of another or ever allow them again. It acknowledges that no matter how much we may have suffered, we will not put another human being out of our heart. We have all been harmed, just as we have all, at times, harmed ourselves and others.

For most people, forgiveness is a process. The work of forgiveness goes through many stages, during which you may feel grief, rage, sorrow, fear, and confusion. In the end, when you let yourself feel the pain you carry, forgiveness comes as a relief, as a release for your heart. You will see that forgiveness is fundamentally for your own sake, a way to let go of the pain of the past.

To practice forgiveness meditation, let yourself sit comfortably, allowing your eyes to close and your breath to be natural and easy. Let your body and mind relax. Breathing gently into the area of your heart, let yourself feel all the barriers you have erected and the emotions that you have carried because you have not forgiven—not forgiven yourself, not forgiven others. Let yourself feel the pain of keeping your heart closed. Then, breathing softly, begin asking and extending forgiveness, reciting the following words, letting the images and feelings that come up grow deeper as you repeat them.

FORGIVENESS OF OTHERS: *There are many ways that I have hurt and harmed others, have betrayed or abandoned them, caused them suffering, knowingly or unknowingly, out of my pain, fear, anger, and confusion.* Let yourself remember and visualize the ways you have hurt others. See and feel the pain you have caused out of your own fear and confusion. Feel your own sorrow and regret. Sense that finally you can release this burden and ask for forgiveness. Picture each memory that still burdens your heart. And then to each person in your mind repeat: *I ask for your forgiveness, I ask for your forgiveness.*

FORGIVENESS FOR YOURSELF: *There are many ways that I have hurt and harmed myself. I have betrayed or abandoned myself many times through thought, word, or deed, knowingly and unknowingly.* Feel your own precious body and life. Let yourself see the ways you have hurt or harmed yourself. Picture them, remember them. Feel the sorrow you have carried from this and sense that you can release these burdens. Extend forgiveness for each of them, one by one. Repeat to yourself: *For the ways I have hurt myself through action or inaction, out of fear, pain, and confusion, I now extend a full and heartfelt forgiveness. I forgive myself, I forgive myself.*

FORGIVENESS FOR THOSE WHO HAVE HURT OR HARMED YOU: *There are many ways I have been harmed by others, abused or abandoned, knowingly or unknowingly, in thought, word, or deed.* Let yourself picture and remember these many ways. Feel the sorrow you have carried from this past and sense that you can release this burden of pain by extending forgiveness when your heart is ready. Now say to yourself: *I now remember the many ways others have hurt or harmed me, wounded me, out of fear, pain, confusion, and anger. I have carried this pain in my heart too long. To the extent that I am ready, I offer them forgiveness. To those who have caused me harm, I offer my forgiveness, I forgive you.*

Let yourself gently repeat these three directions for forgiveness until you feel a release in your heart. For some great pains you may not feel a release but only the burden and the anguish or anger you have held. Touch this softly. Be forgiving of yourself for not being ready to let go and move on. Forgiveness cannot be forced; it cannot be artificial. Simply continue the practice and let the words and images work gradually in their own way. In time you can make the forgiveness meditation a regular part of your life, letting go of the past and opening your heart to each new moment with a wise loving kindness.

COMPASSION MEDITATION

The human heart has the extraordinary capacity to hold and transform the sorrows of life into a great stream of compassion. Compassion is the movement of concern and kindness in response to the difficulty of any living being. Compassion arises when you allow your heart to be touched by the pain and need of another.

To cultivate compassion, let yourself sit still in a centered and quiet way. Breathe softly and feel your body, your heartbeat, the life within you. Feel how you treasure your own life, how you guard yourself in the face of your sorrows. After some time, bring to mind someone close to you whom you dearly love. Picture them and feel your caring for them. Notice how you can hold them in your heart. Then let yourself be aware of their sorrows, their measure of suffering in life. Feel how your heart opens naturally, moving toward them to wish them well, to extend comfort, to share in their pain and meet it with compassion.

This is the natural response of the heart. Along with this response, begin to wish them well, reciting the phrases, *May you be free from pain and sorrow, may you be at peace,* while holding them in your heart of compassion.

After you learn to feel your deep caring for this person close to you, turn your compassionate heart toward yourself. For a time recite the phrases, *May I be free of pain and sorrow, may I be at peace.* Then, one person at a time, extend your compassion to others you know. Picture your loved ones, one at a time. Hold the image of each in your heart and be aware of their difficulties and wish them well. *May you be free from pain and sorrow, may you be at peace.* After this you can gradually open your compassion further, to neighbors, and all those who live far away, and finally to the brotherhood and sisterhood of all beings.

Let yourself feel how the beauty of every being brings you joy and how the suffering of any being makes you weep. Feel your tenderhearted connection with all life and its creatures, how it moves with their sorrows and holds them in compassion.

Now let your heart become a transformer for the sorrows of the world. Feel your breath in the area of your heart, as if you could breathe gently in and out of your heart. Feel the kindness of your heart and envision that with each breath you can touch the pain of others and breathe out compassion. With each out-breath wish all living beings well, extend your caring and merciful heart to them. After some time, sit quietly and let your breath and heart rest naturally as a center of compassion in the midst of the world.

ACKNOWLEDGMENTS

With acknowledgment and gratitude for those words from the Buddha and those words taken literally or in the spirit of meditation masters: Achaan Chaa (pp. 81, 86, 118), Robert Aitkin Roshi (p. 29), Angarika Sujata (p. 30), Azuki (p. 52), Ruth Denison (p. 116), Eihei Dogen (p. 17), Thich Hhat Nhah (pp. 97, 98), Mahaghosananda (pp. 20, 114), Master Mian (pp. 43, 69), Paul Reps (p. 32), Master Rinzai (p. 26), Master Sengstan (pp. 66, 103), Shunryu Suzuki Roshi (pp. 9, 23), Eido Tai Shimano Roshi (p. 123).

For further instructions on the Buddha's way consult:

A Path With Heart, JACK KORNFIELD

Zen Mind, Beginner's Mind, SHUNRYU SUZUKI ROSHI

Peace Is Every Step, THICH NHAT HANH

The Ocean of Wisdom, THE DALAI LAMA

The Tibetan Book of Living and Dying, SOGYAL RINPOCHE

JACK KORNFIELD was trained as a Buddhist monk in Thailand, Burma, and India and has taught meditation worldwide since 1974. He is one of the key teachers to introduce Theravada Buddhist practice to the West. For many years his work has been focused on integrating and bringing alive the great Eastern spiritual teachings in an accessible way for Western students and Western society. Jack also holds a Ph.D. in clinical psychology. He is a husband, father, psychotherapist, and founding teacher of the Insight Meditation Society and the Spirit Rock Center. His books include *A Path with Heart, Seeking the Heart of Wisdom, A Still Forest Pool,* and *Stories of the Spirit, Stories of the Heart.*